Little Rita Rizzo

The Life of Mother Mary Angelica

Barbara A. Gaskell

St. Raphael Center, Inc

Canton, Ohio

St. Raphael Center, Inc/ Mother Angelica Museum
4365 Fulton Drive N.W.   Canton, Ohio 44718
www.CatholicBook.net
www.MotherAgelicaMuseum.com

Little Rita Rizzo/ Barbara A. Gaskell – 1st ed.
ISBN: 978-1-7336090-3-6

This book is dedicated to children who have grown up without a father in the home, who have seen violence in the streets or who have been ostracized because they are different. May these children come to know through this biography that God sees you in your loneliness and He loves you more than you can ever imagine.

Dear Parents and Teachers

"Little Rita Rizzo" is a children's adaptation of "The Amazing Life of Rita Rizzo" which was published in 2019. This book is written to inspire youngsters to love God, overcome obstacles and strive for greatness.

Rita Rizzo, the future Mother Angelica didn't seek worldly fame, she endeavored to know, love, and serve God and become the person He intended her to be. May this simple book inspire all of us to follow her example.

Baby Rita and Mother Mae

Beginnings

Rita Antoinette Rizzo was born on April 20, 1923, in a poor section of Canton, Ohio two blocks north of the railroad tracks. Her father, John, was a tailor born in Italy and her mother, Mae was a housewife. Rita was the couple's first and only child.

Rita's parents had an explosive relationship. John Rizzo was an abusive husband. He was verbally, mentally and physically abusive to his wife Mae. A month after the birth of their daughter Rita, John beat his wife severely. Before Rita was five years old John abandoned his family. He ran away to California with a young woman.

Rita at six years old

School Years

Young Rita and her mother were heart-broken. They had no source of income, so they went to live with Mae's parents.

Grandma and Grandpa Gianfrancesco owned a family friendly tavern that was attached to their home in the southeast end of Canton. Mae's brothers Peter, Nick and Frank also lived in the family home. It made for very crowded quarters.

Rita's mother, Mae filed for divorce and after it was official she enrolled Rita in St. Anthony Catholic School. The school was two blocks away from her grandparents' house.

Life was very hard for young Rita. Many people made fun of her and looked down on her because her family was broken.

Father John Riccardi

Father Riccardi

The pastor of St. Anthony Catholic Church was Father John Riccardi. He was a good priest and shepherd to his people. Father was fighting crime in the neighborhood making it safer for the parish family.

One Sunday when Father Riccardi was getting ready for a baptism, a very bad criminal shot him. He died several hours later. The St. Anthony parish family was devastated.

Father Riccardi was loved not only by his parish family but by many in the community because of his good work. The entire city of Canton was in shock at this evil event. It was a national news sensation.

Rita felt lost. Her father was gone and now her pastor was dead. She wondered how God could let this happen.

CHAPTER 4

The Suffering

Rita and her mother moved out of her grandparents' house because of conflict. After that they moved often from place to place.

A heavy depression fell on Rita's mother who cried every day before Rita left for school. It was hard for Rita to concentrate on schoolwork because she was worried about her mother's mental health and their financial problems.

Rita helped her mother as much as possible with the dry-cleaning business they had started to bring in a little money.

Life was difficult. Rita was sad and frustrated. She just wanted a normal family like the other kids she knew in the neighborhood.

High School

By the time Rita was a freshman in high school, her mother was close to a nervous break-down and finances forced them to move back to her grandparents' house.

One of Rita's teachers invited her to become a drum majorette, so she took up baton twirling. She became so good at twirling that she gave lessons at a local music store. Rita's earnings provided extra income.

Rita's nerves were frayed. She tried to balance her studies, her work and caring for her mother. Mae suffered a nervous breakdown and went to visit her sister Rose in Philadelphia. Rita's grades suffered. By the end of the school year, she had flunked several classes and needed to attend summer school. Rita's majorette days were fin-ished.

Rhoda Wise

The Illness

During her junior year in high school Rita began having terrible stomach problems. Sometimes the pain was so bad that she doubled over in agony. She was unable to eat. By her senior year Rita had lost twenty pounds. The doctors tried many treatments, but nothing helped.

Rita graduated and landed a job, but her stomach problems got worse. Her stomach area began to turn blue, and a large lump appeared.

Mae was desperate to help her daughter. One afternoon Mae shared her deep concerns about Rita with a friend. Her friend encouraged Mae to take Rita to see Rhoda Wise, a local woman who had been miraculously healed by Jesus a few years earlier. Mae contacted Mrs. Wise and they visited her that very evening.

St. Thérèse

The Healing

Rita Rizzo met Rhoda Wise that very evening. Mrs. Wise gave Rita a novena (nine days of prayer) to St. Therese of Lisieux and told Rita to pray the novena to obtain a cure for her stomach ailment. Rita did as instructed and nine days later she was completely healed!

Everything changed for Rita Rizzo from that point forward.

Later in life the future Mother Angelica would say, *"When the Lord came and healed me I had a different attitude. I knew there was a God and that he loved me. I didn't know that before. After I was healed, all I wanted to do was give my life to Jesus."*

CHAPTER 8

Vocation

After her healing Rita began to pray more and asked God to show her how to love Him. One day during prayer Rita felt a strong call from God to give her life to Jesus as a nun. She entered the Poore Clare convent in Cleveland. Her mother Mae was very unhappy about her decision, but Rita persisted.

Rita had problems with swollen knees during her first months in the monastery. Several times the Mother Superior threatened to send her home. Instead, Rita was sent to a monastery in Canton, where there were fewer stairs to climb.

Upon arriving at the new monastery her knees were completely healed. Rita professed final vows and was given the name Sister Angelica. Rita was happy to begin her new life as a Sister of Perpetual Adoration.

The Injury

Sister Angelica began to emerge as a born leader in the small group of nuns in Canton. She oversaw many projects with great enthusiasm.

One day when Sister Angelica was using a floor scrubbing machine, it kicked sideways and knocked Sister Angelica against the wall.

The injury caused her great pain. Two years of limping misery passed. Doctors tried traction, shots in the spine, even a full body cast. Finally, the decision was made for back surgery. Sister Angelica was 33 years old.

The surgeon informed her there was a fifty-fifty chance she would never walk again. Sister Angelica was terrified. At that moment she made a solemn promise to God, "If You let me walk again, I will build You a monastery in the South."

Little Michael uses
St. Peter's Fishing Lures

Did you know that the first fishing lure was made by a Benedictine Nun? Yes, centuries ago a Nun made a lure for casting. We have decided to follow in her footsteps — only we're Franciscans — in fact, we're cloistered Franciscans. But like the good Benedictine Nun we are making fishing lures and we'd be so pleased if you tried them.

The purpose of course is to raise funds to aid the Great Fisherman in His quest for souls. With every lure goes a prayer that He will bless your fishing.

Fishermen tell us that St. Peter's Fishing Lures are the best and we like to believe them. Won't you try them? Enclosed is an envelope for your convenience. Please enclose cash, check, or money order (— sorry, no C.O.D.'s) with your order.

Happy Fishing And Keep Close To The Great Fisherman!

St. Peter's Fishing Lures - Franciscan Nuns
4200 N. Market Ave - Canton 4, Ohio.

Going South

After the surgery Sr. Angelica was sent home with a back brace and crutches, walking with great difficulty. She told her Mother Superior about her vow to build a monastery in the South, explaining her promise to God the night before her operation.

Many obstacles were in the path of young Sister Angelica to fulfill her dream but she was determined.

After much delay, the local bishop finally gave approval to her request but with the stipulation that the new monastery must be able to support itself. Sister Angelica had the idea of selling fishing lures to local anglers to raise money. With the blessing of her Mother Superior, Sister Angelica launched "St. Peter's Fishing Lures."

CHAPTER 11

Our Lady of the Angels

The Sisters raised $13,000 with the fishing lure venture, the exact amount needed to buy a 15-acre plot in Irondale, Alabama, a suburb of Birmingham. Five Sisters from Canton moved to Alabama in 1961. They rented a small house and began building. Soon a woman from Canton asked to join the new community of nuns; her name was Mae Francis. Mother Angelica's own mother became a nun!

As word spread about the building of the monastery donors came forward with great generosity. Bricks, concrete, flooring, monetary donations all began to pour in. Even the construction workers donated their time and talent.

Our Lady of the Angels Monastery in Irondale, Alabama was dedicated May 20, 1962.

to leave and yet to stay
IHS
BY MOTHER M. ANGELICA
HIS PAIN—LIKE MINE
BY MOTHER M. ANGELICA
MINI-BOOK
SPIRITUAL HANGOVERS
MINI-BOOK
MY MOTHER - the church
KNOWING GOD'S WILL
BY MOTHER M. ANGELICA
MINI-BOOK
I AM his temple
BY MOTHER M. ANGELICA
MINI-BOOK
In Praise of Goodness
BY MOTHER M. ANGELICA
OK
IN THE SHADOW OF HIS LIGHT
BY Mother M. Angelica
MINI-BOOK

Mini-books

In 1971 Mother Angelica was given permission by her bishop to accept local speaking engagements. Her popularity as a faith-filled, yet entertaining speaker grew.

Mother Angelica began writing short teachings about the Bible and the Catholic Faith in front of the Blessed Sacrament. The community decided to turn these teachings into mini books. A local radio station aired short segments that Mother Angelica recorded.

By 1976 Mother Angelica had written 50 mini books. The mini books became so popular that the Sisters bought a printing press and printed the books in-house shipping them worldwide. She also recorded hundreds of teachings which were made available to the public.

Mother Angelica starts her own television network

CHAPTER 13

Television

When television networks began to request interviews, Mother Angelica realized she could reach a tremendous number of souls through television.

In 1978 Mother Angelica began recording a series named "The Hermitage" to be sent across the nation. The local TV station where she recorded her show planned to air a blasphemous movie. Mother scolded the president of the studio. He dismissed her concern. She made an ultimatum that if he aired the movie, she would never come to his studio again. He laughed at her and said she needed him. Mother told him that she would not be back but that she would build her own studio.

EWTN

After her encounter with the studio executive, Mother Angelica went back to her monastery in great distress. Her sisters supported her decision. The community prayed that God would show them a way forward.

The monastery had recently begun building a new garage. The Sisters made the decision to expand the garage building and make a television studio instead.

The community had no money, no knowledge of television and no long-term plan but they knew that God would lead them. That day the seed of the Eternal Word Television Network (EWTN) was planted. The seed sprouted and the little sapling grew by grace, prayer, determination and hard work into what is now the largest Catholic media network in the world!

CHAPTER 15

History of Accomplishments

1981 Mother Angelica was the first woman to apply for and receive an FCC license for satellite television. EWTN became the first Catholic satellite television station in the United States.

Mother Angelica founded three religious orders, the Franciscan Missionaries of the Eternal Word for men, and Sister Servants of the Eternal Word for women in 1987. Then in 1998 she founded the Knights of the Holy Eucharist.

1992: Mother Angelica launched WEWN, the largest privately owned international short wave radio network with a potential listening audience of 600 million souls.

1995: TIME Magazine names Mother Angelica as the Most Influential Roman Catholic Woman in the United States.

1996: Mother Angelica receives a miraculous message from the Divine Child Jesus, "Build Me a Temple, and I will help those who help you."

1997: EWTN offers radio programs free of charge to any AM/FM radio outlet.

1998: Mother Angelica is healed of her back and leg ailments while praying with Paola Albertini, an Italian mystic.

1999: The Shrine of the Most Blessed Sacrament of Our Lady of the Angels Monastery in Hanceville, Alabama is consecrated. Price tag: $35 million. The $35 million was donated by 5 donors.

2003: Mother Angelica is inducted into the Cable TV Pioneer Class of 2003

2004: Alabama Broadcasters Association names Mother Angelica "Citizen of the Year."

2009: Mother Angelica is awarded the "Pro Ecclessia et Pontifice" by Pope Benedict XVI: the highest honor a Pope can bestow.

March 27, 2016: Mother Angelica died at her monastery in Hanceville, Alabama.

The above image is the copyright of St. Raphael Center

May not be reproduced without permission

"I live because of the Eucharist."

Mother Angelica